Learning Playground

Fun with Shapes

WORLD
BOOK

a Scott Fetzer company
Chicago

www.worldbookonline.com

World Book, Inc.
233 N. Michigan Avenue
Chicago, IL 60601
U.S.A.

For information about other World Book publications,
visit our Web site at **http://www.worldbookonline.com**
or call **1-800-WORLDBK (967-5325).**

For information about sales to schools and libraries, call
1-800-975-3250 (United States);
1-800-837-5365 (Canada).

Library of Congress Cataloging-in-Publication Data

Fun with shapes.
    p. cm. -- (Learning playground)
  Includes index.
  Summary: "An activity-based volume that introduces
early concepts in geometry. Features include a glossary,
an additional resource list, and an index"-- Provided by
publisher.
  ISBN 978-0-7166-0229-3
  1. Shapes--Juvenile literature. I. World Book, Inc.
QA445.5.F86 2011
516'.15--dc23
                    2011017694

STAFF
Executive Committee
President: Donald D. Keller
Vice President and
   Editor in Chief: Paul A. Kobasa
Vice President, Marketing/
   Digital Products: Sean Klunder
Vice President, International: Richard Flower
Director, Human Resources: Bev Ecker

Editorial
Associate Manager, Supplementary
   Publications: Cassie Mayer
Editor: Daniel Kenis
Researcher: Annie Brodsky
Manager, Contracts & Compliance
   (Rights & Permissions): Loranne K. Shields
Indexer: David Pofelski

Graphics and Design
Manager: Tom Evans
Coordinator, Design Development and
   Production: Brenda B. Tropinski
Associate Designer: Matt Carrington
Photographs Editor: Kathy Creech

Pre-Press and Manufacturing
Director: Carma Fazio
Manufacturing Manager: Barbara Podczerwinski
Production/Technology Manager:
   Anne Fritzinger

Learning Playground
Set ISBN: 978-0-7166-0225-5

Printed in Malaysia by TWP Sdn Bhd, Johor Bahru
1st printing July 2011

Acknowledgments:
The publishers gratefully acknowledge the following sources for photography. All illustrations
were prepared by WORLD BOOK unless otherwise noted.

Cover: Dreamstime; iStockphoto; Shutterstock

Klaus Mellenthin, Westend61/Alamy Images 43; Dreamstime 4, 19, 26, 38, 52; Shutterstock
4, 5, 8, 9, 10, 11, 12, 13, 14, 15, 18, 30, 39, 40, 41, 48, 52, 53; Audrey Tropinski 46-47.

Table of Contents

There is a glossary on page 62. Terms defined in the glossary are in type that **looks like this** on their first appearance on any spread (two facing pages).

Shapes Everywhere

Some board games have shapes, such as the squares on a chessboard.

Balls are in the shape of a sphere.

Rectangle

Square

Circle

Triangle

Think of all the shapes in your world! Your toys and games, for example, are made up of many shapes. The face of a checkerboard has many squares. The top of a checker is a circle. A sail on a toy boat is in the shape of a triangle.

Look for shapes in other things you use. A book cover is a rectangle. A DVD is a circle. What other shapes can you find?

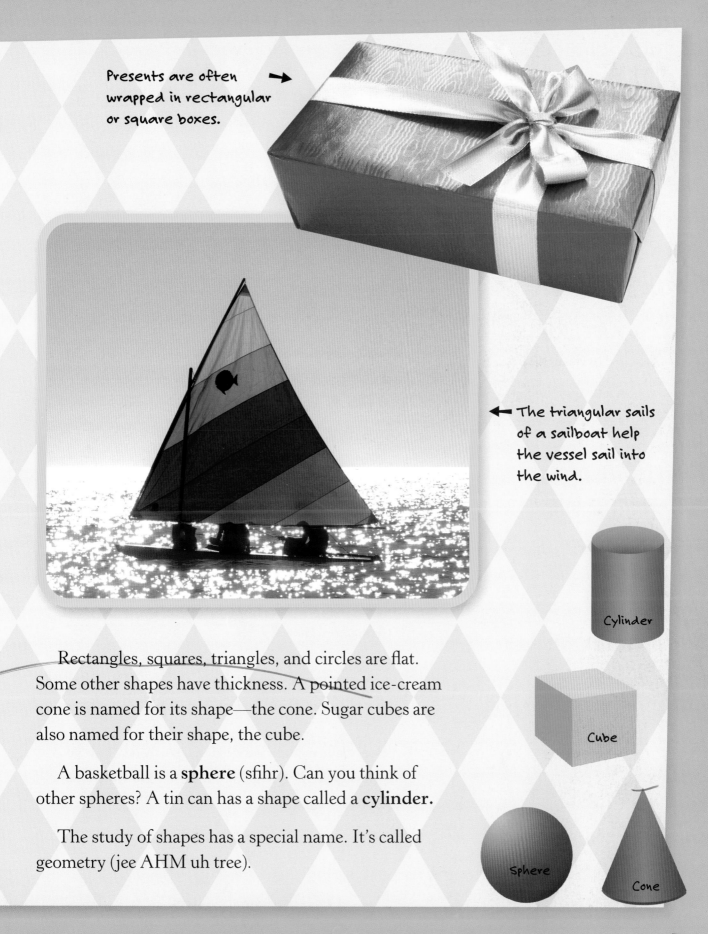

Presents are often wrapped in rectangular or square boxes. →

← The triangular sails of a sailboat help the vessel sail into the wind.

Cylinder

Cube

Rectangles, squares, triangles, and circles are flat. Some other shapes have thickness. A pointed ice-cream cone is named for its shape—the cone. Sugar cubes are also named for their shape, the cube.

A basketball is a **sphere** (sfihr). Can you think of other spheres? A tin can has a shape called a **cylinder.**

The study of shapes has a special name. It's called geometry (jee AHM uh tree).

Sphere

Cone

SHAPE TANGLE

Here's a game with a special twist!
You can play it with your friends.

MATERIALS
- Construction paper
- Scissors
- Masking tape

DIRECTIONS

1. Cut three squares, three circles, and three triangles out of the construction paper. The shapes should be a little larger than the size of your hand. You can use different colors for the shapes.

2. Find two or more friends to play with you. The more players you have, the more fun the game will be!

3. Hold the shapes over your head and drop them.

4. Tape the shapes to the floor where they land. (Ask permission first!)

5. Pick one player to be the "caller." The rest of the players should stand around the shapes.

6. The caller gives directions, such as "Put your elbow on a square," or "Touch your right knee to a triangle."

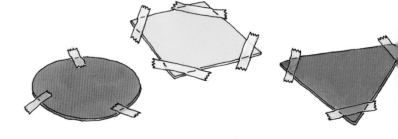

7. The other players must follow the directions. The first one or two will be easy, but after that, players usually must bend and twist to reach several shapes at once. Two or more players can touch the same shapes.

8. Players who fall down or cannot follow a direction are out of the game. The winning player gets to be the caller for the next game!

Lines and Points

What is between this sentence and the next one? ——————————

You probably said, "It's a line." Lines are everywhere. People use lines to mark such things as highway lanes, parking spaces, and the days on a calendar.

But what is a line? It's a long, thin mark. It can be straight or curved. A straight line is the shortest distance between two points.

A point has no length or width. It only has a position. To show its position, we can draw a dot: ●

Lines are all around you. Streets have painted lines to show pedestrian crosswalks.

Lines are used to show the boundaries in many sports games.

In real life, lines end. You can measure the length of a line. These lines are called line segments. But in geometry, you can imagine a line that goes on forever. It's impossible to draw a line that goes on forever. But you can symbolize such a line by adding arrows to both ends of a line segment:

We can also draw a line that stops at one end and goes on forever in the other direction. This kind of line is called a **ray**:

Some lines are always the same distance from each other. They never meet, no matter how far you extend them. They are called **parallel** lines.

Try this!

Train tracks are parallel lines. They are always the same distance from each other and never meet.

You can use dots and lines to make a picture like the one to the right. All you need are paper and a pencil or marker. Think of a shape—for example, a rectangle. Draw four dots for the corners. Then connect them with straight lines.

Now turn your rectangle into part of a bigger picture, like a house. Draw more dots to show the outline of the picture. Then connect them with straight lines.

You can even make a dot picture for a friend to finish! Draw dots for the outline. Number the dots to show which ones should be connected. Let your friend draw lines from dot to dot, starting with 1.

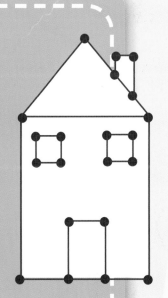

Angles

When two lines meet at a point, they make an **angle.** You've probably seen angles in many objects around you. Look at the face of a clock. Do you see how the two hands form an angle? What about the angles that are formed at the corners of the book shown below?

The hands of a clock form different angles throughout the day.

90°

Right angle

Angles can look quite different from one another. Some angles are so wide that they almost make a straight line. Others are so narrow that their two **rays** nearly touch. We can measure angles using a tool called a **protractor.**

The size of an angle is measured in degrees. Angles are measured from the vertex—the point where two rays meet.

Some angles have special names. In a **right angle,** the two rays make a square corner. Right angles are always 90 degrees. Take a look at the edges of the book again. Do you see the right angles?

An **acute angle** is any angle that measures less than 90 degrees. Acute angles look like jaws that are starting to close.

Obtuse angles are always more than 90 degrees. They look like jaws that are open wide!

Acute angle

Obtuse angle

Try this!

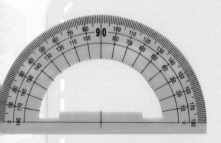

A protractor is a tool for measuring the size of angles or for drawing angles of different sizes. Most protractors are shaped like the letter D, with the arc in the shape of a semicircle. Lines and numbers on the arc indicate angles from 0 to 180 degrees.

Try using a protractor to measure the angles of different shapes, such as the corners of a book. You can also draw examples of angles and then measure them. To measure an angle, line up the straight edge of the protractor—or the line printed on it—along one line of the angle. Look at the number on the protractor that appears where the other line crosses the arc. This is the measurement of the angle.

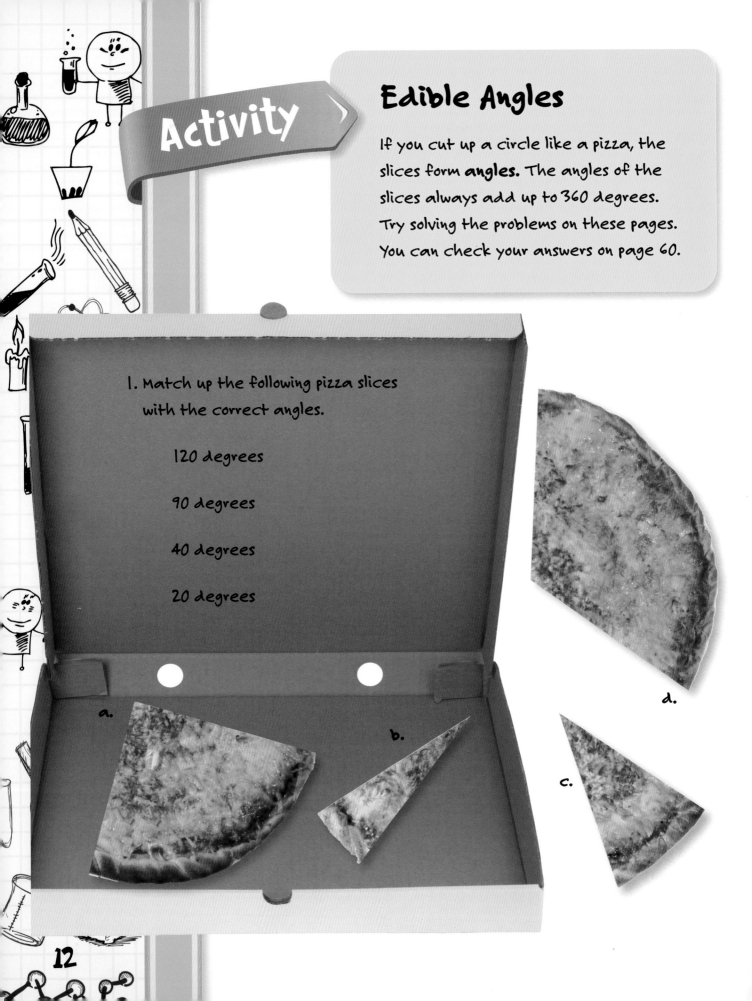

Edible Angles

If you cut up a circle like a pizza, the slices form **angles**. The angles of the slices always add up to 360 degrees. Try solving the problems on these pages. You can check your answers on page 60.

1. Match up the following pizza slices with the correct angles.

   120 degrees

   90 degrees

   40 degrees

   20 degrees

a.

b.

c.

d.

2. If you add these slices together, you would need one more of which slice to make a complete 360-degree pizza?

3. Which slice could you use three of to make a complete circle?

What other combinations of these slices can make a circle? You can trace the shapes onto a piece of paper and cut them out to help you figure this out.

Triangles

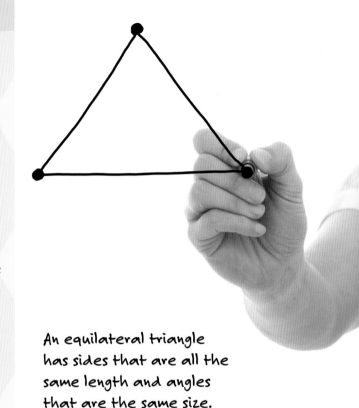

An **angle** has two sides. If you add a third side, you get a shape called a triangle (TRY ang guhl). Triangles have three straight sides and three angles. The word *triangle* means "three angles."

An **equilateral** (ee kwuh LAT uhr uhl) triangle is a special kind of triangle. Its sides are all the same length. Its angles are all the same size. The word *equilateral* means "equal sided."

An equilateral triangle has sides that are all the same length and angles that are the same size.

An **isosceles** (y SOS uh leez) triangle has at least two equal sides. All equilateral triangles are isosceles—but not all isosceles are equilateral!

Isosceles triangle

Try this!

Make a picture. Start with angles and triangles. Then add details to finish your picture. What did you make?

Some triangles have no two sides that are the same. They're called **scalene** (skay LEEN) triangles.

Scalene triangle

Some triangles are named for their angles. Take a look at the triangle to the right. It has a **right angle,** so it's called a **right triangle.** Right triangles always have one angle that measures 90 degrees.

Right triangle

How many triangles do you see on this house?

15

COUNTING TRIANGLES

The design on this page is made of 88 triangles. Can you find them all? Cover the next page while you look!

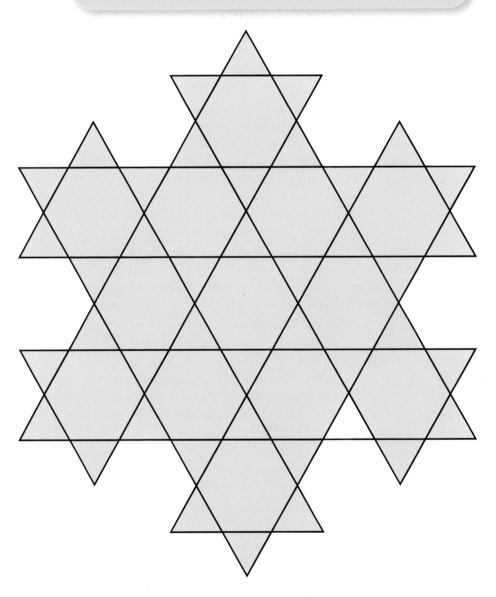

Here's one more question for you: What kind of triangle are they?

You can check your answer on page 60.

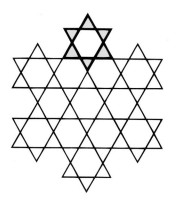

There are 42 triangles of this size. They point in all directions.

There are 26 triangles of this size, 13 pointing up and 13 pointing down.

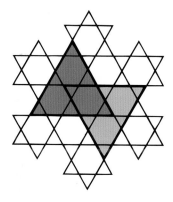

There are 12 triangles of this size, 6 pointing up and 6 pointing down.

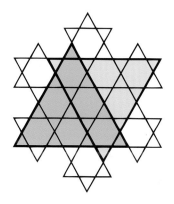

There are 6 triangles of this size, 3 pointing up and 3 pointing down.

Finally, there are 2 triangles of this size, 1 pointing up and 1 pointing down.

That makes a total of 88 triangles. Did you find them all?

Four-Sided Shapes

Many objects around us have four sides. Can you name some four-sided shapes? You may have a picture on your wall that has four sides. What about your door? Or a television? A piece of paper has four sides, too.

Many objects around the home are four-sided. How many squares and rectangles do you see in this picture?

A square is a shape with four sides and four corners. All sides of a square are the same length. And all of its **angles** are **right angles.** They measure 90 degrees.

Square

Rectangles are also four-sided shapes. They have four right angles. And they have two sets of equal sides. The opposite sides of a rectangle are equal in length.

Some four-sided shapes look like squares that are leaning to one side. This kind of shape is called a **rhombus.**

A rhombus has four equal sides. Its opposite sides are **parallel**. They are also equal in length.

A **parallelogram** is similar to a rhombus. Its opposite sides are parallel and equal in length. And its opposite angles are equal.

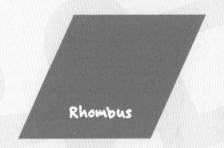

Rectangle

Rhombus

Parallelogram

What shape does the side of this office building resemble?

19

DISAPPEARING SQUARES

As you have learned, a square is a shape with four equal sides. Use four toothpicks, stirring sticks, or straws to make a square. Now try to solve these square puzzles.

MATERIALS

- 17 toothpicks, stirring sticks, or straws

DIRECTIONS

1. Put 17 sticks together to make six squares, like this:

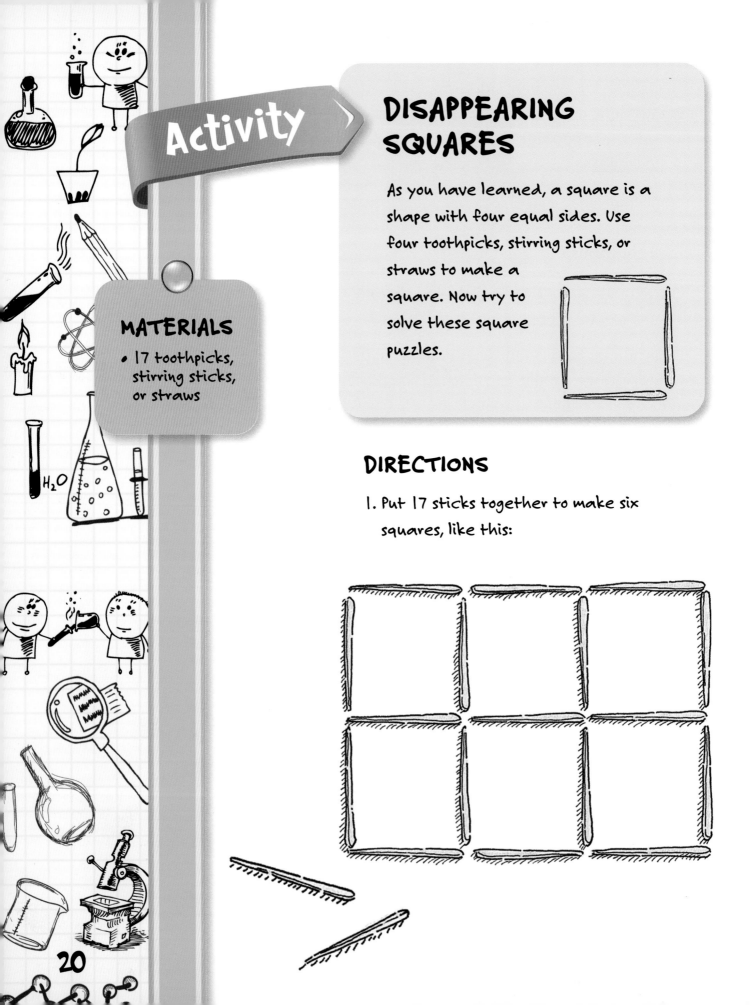

2. Now take away four sticks so that only four squares are left. There's more than one way to solve this puzzle. Can you find at least two solutions?

3. Put your six squares back together. Now take away four sticks so that only three squares are left. (Hint: All the squares don't have to be the same size.)

4. Put 12 sticks together to make a "tic-tac-toe" board like this:

5. Now see if you can:
   a. Make four squares by moving four sticks.
   b. Make three squares by moving four sticks.
   c. Make two squares by moving six sticks.

You can check your solutions on page 60.

Polyominoes

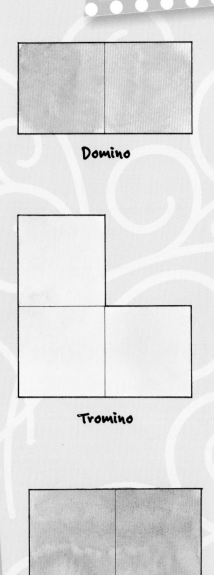

Domino

Tromino

A polyomino (pahl ee AHM uh noh) is a shape made from squares. The squares must be joined by at least one full side.

Polyominoes are named for the number of squares they contain. A domino is a shape made from two squares. Have you ever played a game of dominoes?

Shapes made from three squares are called trominoes. A four-square shape is a tetromino. How many different tetrominoes can you draw?

Shapes made from five squares are called pentominoes (pehn TAHM uh nohz). There are 12 different pentominoes.

Tetromino

Pentominoes

Draw the 12 pentominoes shown on these pages on graph paper (paper with tiny squares all over it). Cut them out. Then fit the pieces together to make a rectangle. You can turn or flip the pieces as needed.

First try making a 6 x 10 rectangle. That's a rectangle with 6 squares on two sides and 10 squares on the other two sides. Then try making a 5 x 12 rectangle.

There are more than a thousand ways to make each rectangle! You will find two solutions on page 60.

Try this!

Square Puzzle

Imagine there's a square with sides that are 100 units long. How could you double the size of the square but still keep it in the shape of a square?

You might first try doubling the sides of the square so that they are 200 units long. They would now be twice as long as the sides of the old square. But now the square is four times as big as your original square!

What if you divided the square into four smaller squares? Then you could add on four new squares that are the same size as the small squares. Try drawing this on a piece of paper. What shape do you see? This makes a rectangle, not a square.

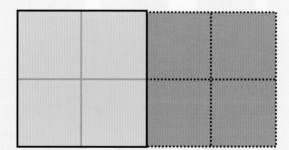

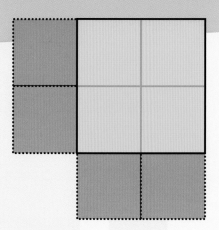

Now try adding two small squares to one side of the old square and two to another side. This almost works, but there is a piece missing out of one corner, so it isn't a perfect square.

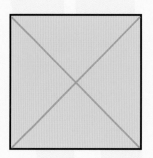

What if you divided the old square into four triangles by drawing lines between the opposite corners? Can you add four more triangles of exactly the same size to your square—and somehow make a bigger square?

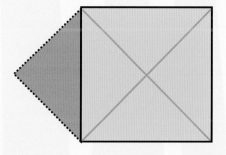

Try adding a triangle to one side of the old square. Then add a triangle to each of the other sides.

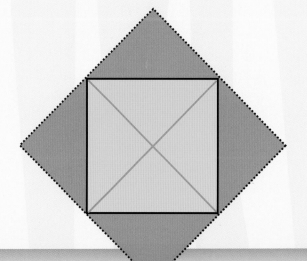

Look at your paper closely. Now turn it sideways. What do you see? A square!

Now you know a secret: You can use triangles to double the size of a square— and still have a square!

The 3-4-5 Triangle

How can you use shapes to measure a field with 90-degree corners? The ancient Egyptians solved this problem.

Triangles and squares work together in other ways, too. Let's say you wanted to measure a plot of land. How could you make a neat, four-sided field with **right angles?** You can't just eyeball it, or your field may look like this:

The ancient Egyptians solved this puzzle thousands of years ago. They discovered a "magic" 3-4-5 triangle. A worker knotted a loop of rope into 12 equal spaces. The worker stretched the rope around three stakes to form a triangle. He placed the stakes so the triangle had sides of 3, 4, and 5 units. The knots in the rope allowed the worker to measure the units.

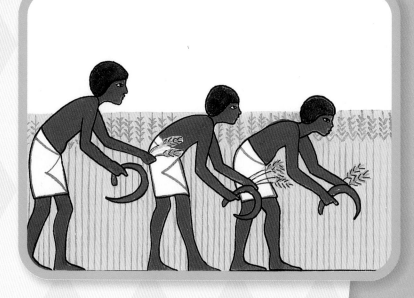

The ancient Egyptians used the 3-4-5 triangle to make fields with 90 degree corners.

The 3-4-5 triangle is a **right triangle.** The longest side—the one that measures 5 units—is called the hypotenuse (hy POT uh noos). And the **angle** opposite the hypotenuse is always a right angle. If you can make a right angle, it's easy to make a field with 90-degree corners!

A rope with 12 knots wraps around 3 posts to make a 3-4-5 triangle.

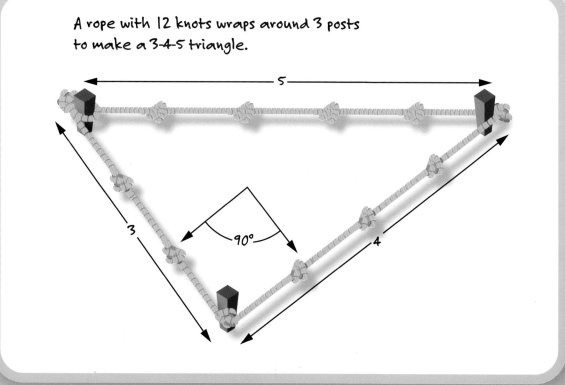

ANGLES OF A TRIANGLE

The three **angles** of every triangle always add up to one straight line of 180 degrees. Here's a simple way to prove it.

MATERIALS

- Paper
- Scissors
- Ruler
- Pencil

DIRECTIONS

1. Use a ruler to help you draw a triangle onto a piece of paper. Any size will do, as long as the sides are straight. Cut out the triangle.

2. Find the longest side of the triangle. Take the point of the angle opposite the longest side and fold it over so that it meets the edge of the longest side. The fold should be **parallel** with the edge.

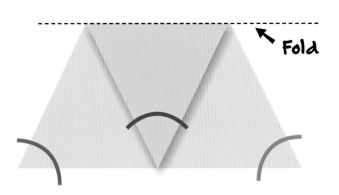

3. Fold the points of the other two angles to meet the point of the folded section. All three points should fit together, with their tips meeting at the same spot.

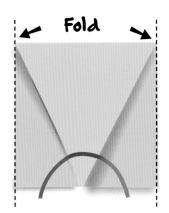

What shape have you made? Notice how the three angles add up to one straight line of 180 degrees along the edge. Now try it again with a different type of triangle. Are there any triangles that do not follow this rule?

180 degrees

Polygons

You can see polygons all around you, such as the squares on a waffle or in a window or the hexagons on a soccer ball.

A **polygon** (PAHL ee gahn) is any flat shape whose sides are straight lines. We have already met some of them. Polygons are named for the number of sides they have.

How many sides does a triangle have? Yes, *tri* means "three."

Square

Rectangle

Triangle

A **quadrilateral** has four sides. (*Quad* means "four.") Rectangles, **rhombuses,** squares, trapezoids, and **parallelograms** are all quadrilaterals.

Trapezoid

Parallelogram

Here are some more polygons:

A pentagon is a five-sided shape.

Here's a nonagon. Count the nine sides.

A hexagon is a six-sided shape.

The octagon has eight sides. It is a familiar shape in many countries because it is used for stop signs.

How many sides does a heptagon have? That's right—seven!

We'll stop with a 10-sided shape. It's called a decagon.

LINES OF SYMMETRY

When two parts of a shape match exactly, they are symmetrical (sih MEHT ruh kuhl). A line that divides a shape into two matching halves is called a line of symmetry.

Some shapes have several lines of symmetry. A square has four lines of symmetry. This is true for any square.

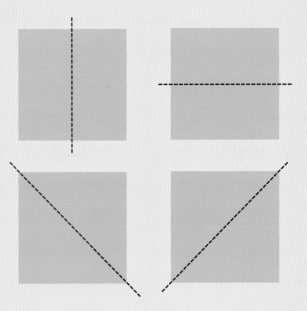

MATERIALS

- Tracing paper
- Pencil
- Construction paper
- Scissors

DIRECTIONS

1. Trace the shapes on the next page. Transfer these shapes to a sheet of construction paper.

2. Cut out the shapes and try different ways of folding them in half. How many lines of symmetry can you find for each shape? (Note: some shapes may have no lines of symmetry.) Answers appear on page 61.

a.

b.

c.

d.

e.

f.

g.

h.

TANGRAMS

The pattern below is made of different shapes. This pattern is called a tangram (TANG gram). It is one of the oldest puzzles in the world. Tangrams were popular in China thousands of years ago.

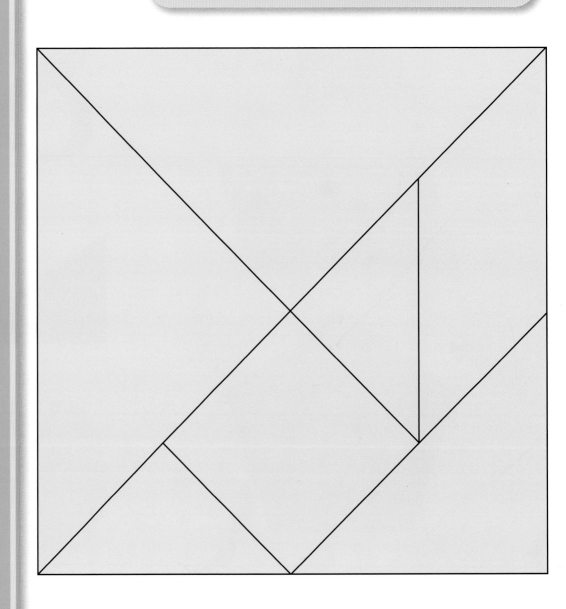

DIRECTIONS

1. Lay your paper over the square on page 34 and trace the lines. Use the ruler to help you draw straight lines.

2. Cut out the seven shapes: two large triangles, two small triangles, one medium triangle, one square, and one **parallelogram,** which looks like a slanted rectangle.

MATERIALS
- Piece of paper
- Scissors
- Pencil
- Ruler

3. Fit all the pieces together to make a rectangle like this one.

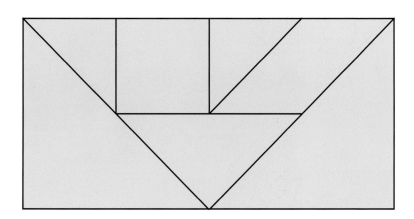

TANGRAMS

4. Now try to make these shapes with your tangram pieces—a dinosaur, a bird, and a steamboat.

5. Make your own shapes with the tangram pieces. What else can you make?

Check your solutions on page 61.

Dinosaur

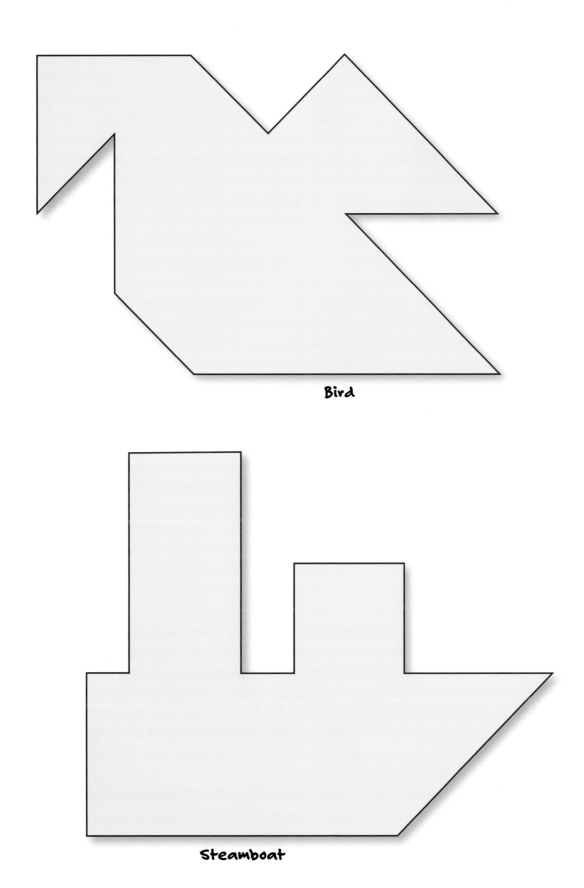

Bird

Steamboat

Decorate with Shapes

Some shapes fit neatly together. We call these shapes tesserae (TEHS uh ree). You may find tesserae in floors and walls. Does your bathroom or kitchen floor have tiles? Those tiles are tesserae.

Squares and triangles are often used to decorate tile floors.

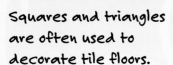

Try this!

A mosaic (moh ZAY ihk) is a decoration made of tiny pieces of clay, glass, or stone. The ancient Romans liked mosaics. The floors and walls of Roman temples and villas were often covered with complicated patterns.

The mosaic shown to the right is made of colorful stones and glass. But you can make your own mosaic out of colored paper or old magazines! Experiment to find out which shapes fit together. Glue your shapes onto a piece of cardboard to make a picture or a design.

Look at the patterns on this page. What shapes do you see?

Some shapes are easy to use as tesserae. For example, square tiles can easily fill a whole floor. So can triangle-shaped tiles. But what about octagon-shaped tiles? You can't fill a floor with just octagons. There would be square-shaped gaps in between the tiles. But if you use both octagon and square tiles, you can fill the whole floor.

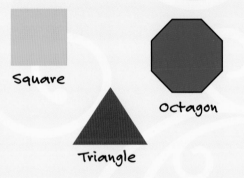

Square

Triangle

Octagon

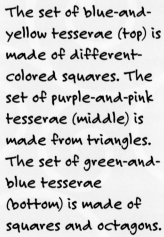

The set of blue-and-yellow tesserae (top) is made of different-colored squares. The set of purple-and-pink tesserae (middle) is made from triangles. The set of green-and-blue tesserae (bottom) is made of squares and octagons.

This ancient Roman floor mosaic shows a partridge perched on a branch.

All points in the curve of a circle are the same distance from the circle's center.

Around and Around

Did you ever ride a Ferris wheel or a carousel? These rides—and many other rides at fairs and amusement parks—are made with circles.

A circle is a closed curve. Every point on the edge of the circle is the same distance from the center. This distance is called the **radius** (RAY dee uhs).

The distance across a circle, going through the center, is called the **diameter** (dy AM uh tuhr). The diameter is always twice as long as the radius.

Radius

Diameter

Circumference

The radius of a circle is half the length of the diameter. The circumference is the distance around the outside of the circle.

The distance around the edge of a circle is called the **circumference** (suhr KUHM fuhr uhns).

There is a special number connected with circles. The number is often written as a Greek letter, π, called pi. It's pronounced like "pie." This number is simply a circle's circumference, divided by its diameter. If you take any circle's circumference and divide it by the diameter, it always equals the same number: about 3.1415. This works for every circle, no matter how big or small.

Many common objects have a circular shape, such as toy disks.

DRAW A CIRCLE

You can easily draw a circle with a tool called a compass. If you don't have a compass, try drawing a circle by following these directions.

MATERIALS

- Piece of paper
- Thick piece of cardboard
- 1 pushpin
- String
- Pencil

DIRECTIONS

1. Lay a piece of paper on the cardboard. Press a pushpin into the center of the paper.

2. Tie one end of a short piece of string, about 4 inches (10 centimeters) long, to the pushpin. Tie the other end of the string around a pencil. Tie the string loosely, but make sure it is tied tight enough that it will not fall off.

3. Stretch out the string and put the tip of the pencil on the paper. Hold the pencil upright. Move the pencil around the pushpin, keeping the string pulled tight. When you reach your starting point, you'll have a circle!

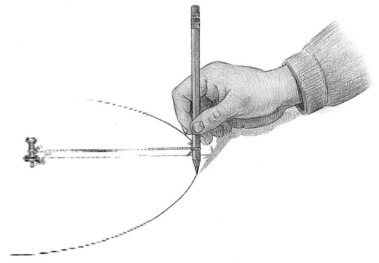

MORE CIRCLE FUN

You can create patterns and decorations using a compass. Here is a simple one to try!

1. Draw a circle.

2. Reduce the size of the compass opening slightly and place the point of the compass on the curve. Draw a partial circle, as shown.

3. Continue to draw circle segments, as shown.

Now you have made a flower inside the circle. Try to make other circular designs!

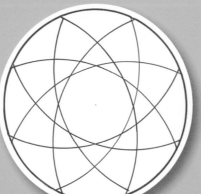

CONGRUENT SHAPES

Activity

By now, you've met many types of shapes, and you know that there are many things that make up a shape. We can describe a shape by the number and length of its sides. We can also measure its **angles.**

When two shapes are exactly the same size and shape, we say that they are congruent (KONG gru uhnt). We can find out if two shapes are congruent by measuring all of their sides and angles.

1. Look at this group of triangles. Can you tell which ones are congruent?

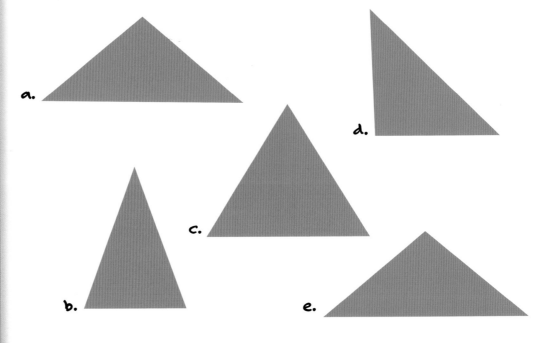

2. Now look at these **quadrilaterals.** How many
   pairs of congruent shapes do you see?

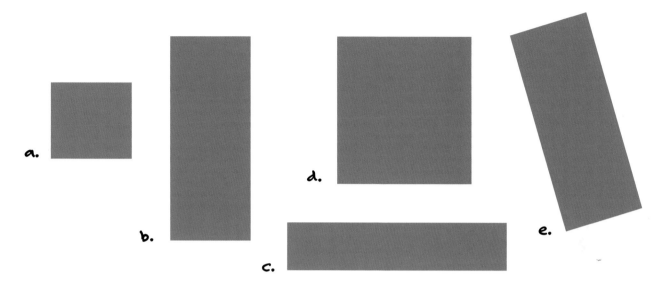

a.

b.

c.

d.

e.

3. What about these **polygons?**

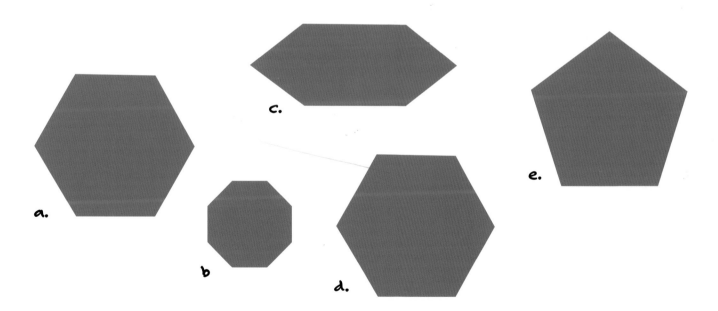

a.

b.

c.

d.

e.

You can check your answers on page 61.

WHAT IS THE PERIMETER?

A **perimeter** is the distance around the edge of an object. You can measure the perimeter of any object using this simple method.

DIRECTIONS

1. Make an outline around an object with the string. Make sure the string stays as close as possible to the edge of the object.

2. Measure how much string you used. This will give you the object's perimeter.

3. You can use this method for many different objects. First, try measuring the perimeter of your hand. Put the palm of your hand flat on a table with your fingers spread out.

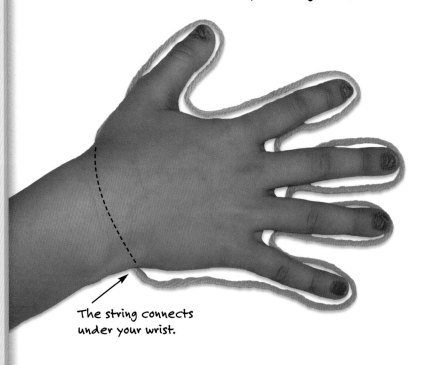

The string connects under your wrist.

4. Place the string around the edge of your fingers and underneath your wrist. (You can also do this by tracing the edge of your hand with a pencil and paper and laying the string over the outline.)

5. Measure how much string was needed. This is the perimeter of your hand!

MATERIALS

- Pencil
- String
- Ruler
- Scissors

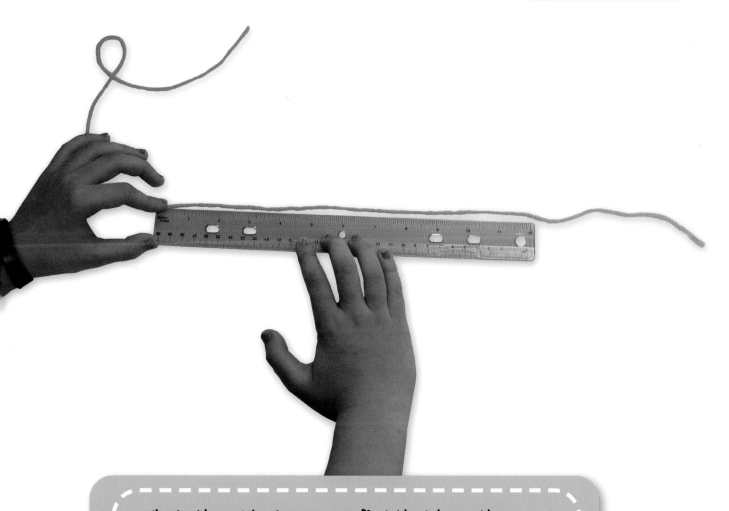

What other objects can you find that have the same perimeter as your hand? Measure a friend's hand. Whose hand has a longer perimeter?

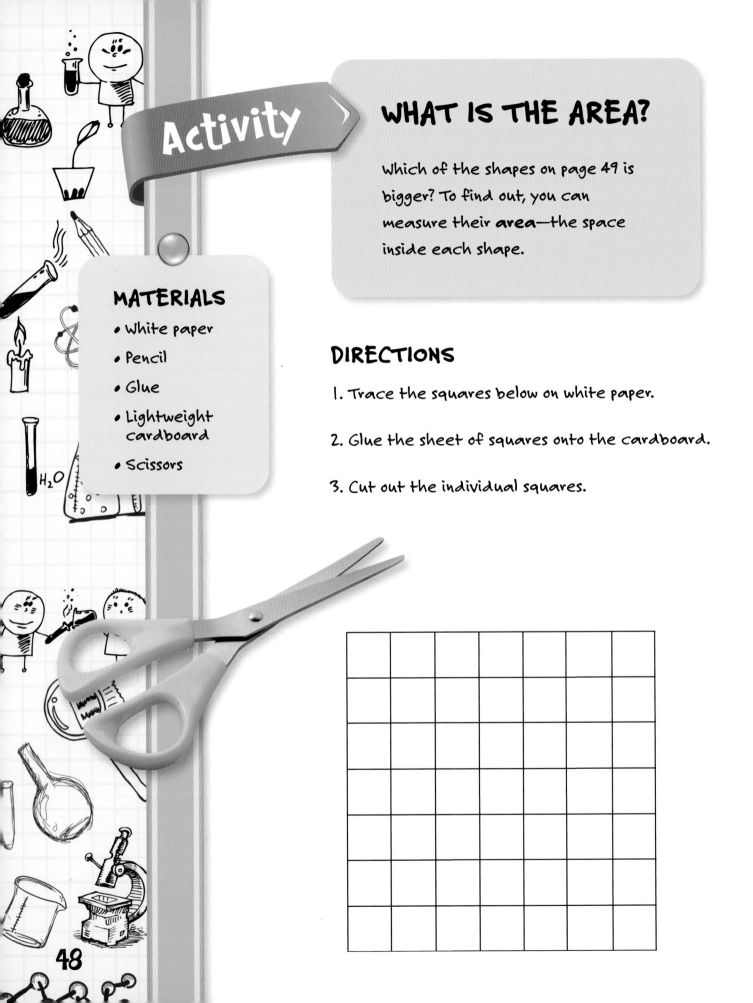

Activity

WHAT IS THE AREA?

Which of the shapes on page 49 is bigger? To find out, you can measure their **area**—the space inside each shape.

MATERIALS

- White paper
- Pencil
- Glue
- Lightweight cardboard
- Scissors

DIRECTIONS

1. Trace the squares below on white paper.

2. Glue the sheet of squares onto the cardboard.

3. Cut out the individual squares.

H_2O

4. Lay the squares inside the castle shown above. Don't leave any space between the squares. How many squares fit inside the castle?

5. Now lay the squares inside the skyscraper to the left. How many squares fit inside it?

6. Compare how many squares you put in the castle with how many you put in the skyscraper. Which number is bigger? That tells you which shape has the greater area!

You can check your answers on page 61.

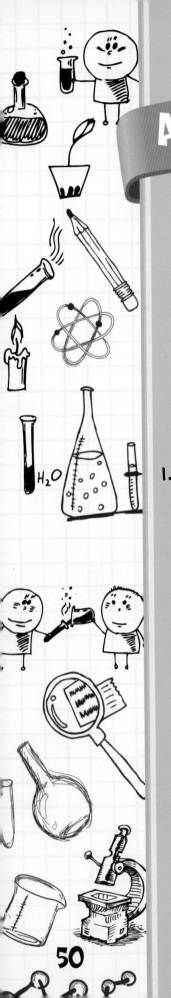

WHAT IS THE AREA?

Look at the square on page 48. Each side has seven square units. What if you wanted to know the exact **area** of the square?

You could count all of the squares inside to find out. There are 49 squares, so the area of the square equals 49 square units. If you wanted to find the area quickly, you could multiply the length of one side by the width of one side. This trick works for all rectangles and squares. Check your answer. Did you get 49?

Try using **multiplication** to find the area of the shapes on these pages. You can check your answers on page 61.

1.

2.

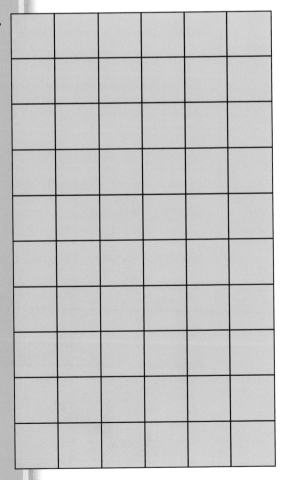

3.

4.

5.

Cone

A party hat
is a cone.

As you know, some shapes are flat and some are not. Squares and circles are flat, but cubes, **spheres, cylinders,** and cones are not.

A flat shape has two dimensions: length and width.

A solid shape has three dimensions: length, width, and height.

Some examples of solid shapes are shown here. Can you find other examples of solid shapes around your home? What about your home itself? What kind of solid shapes make up the shape of your house or apartment building?

Sphere

A baseball is
a sphere.

Cylinder

A can is a
cylinder.

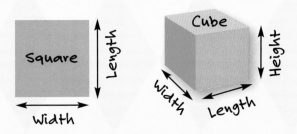

A die is
a cube.

Try this!

A pyramid is a famous solid shape.

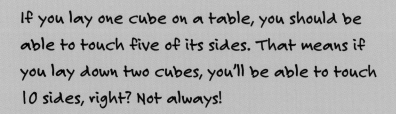

If you lay one cube on a table, you should be able to touch five of its sides. That means if you lay down two cubes, you'll be able to touch 10 sides, right? Not always!

Find a way to lay down two cubes so that you can only touch eight sides. Now try something a little trickier: Lay down three cubes so that only 11 sides can be touched. Here's one last puzzle: Can you lay down four cubes so that only 12 sides can be touched? Check your solutions on page 61.

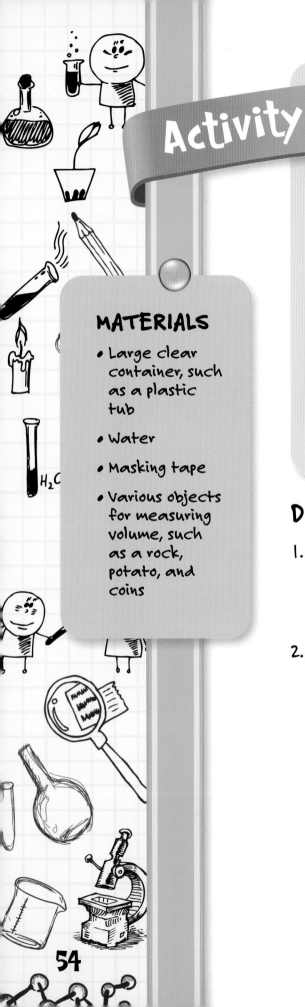

WHAT IS THE VOLUME?

Just as flat shapes have **area**, solid shapes have **volume.** Volume tells how much space solid shapes take up.

Did you ever notice how the water level rises when you get into the bathtub? This is because you have added your volume to the volume of the water. One of the easiest ways to measure the volume of an object is by seeing how much the water level changes when that object is placed underwater.

MATERIALS

- Large clear container, such as a plastic tub

- Water

- Masking tape

- Various objects for measuring volume, such as a rock, potato, and coins

DIRECTIONS

1. Fill the container about three-quarters with water. The water should be about 6 inches (15 centimeters) deep.

2. When the water is still, mark the water level on the outside of the container with the masking tape. The top edge of the tape should be even with the water level.

3. Measure the volume of your hand by making a fist and lowering it into the water up to your wrist. Be very still and let the level of the water settle. Mark the new level with another piece of masking tape. (You may need someone to help you with this). The difference in the water level shows how much volume your fist takes up in the water.

4. Next, try putting various objects in the container to find out which have a volume similar to your fist's. If the water level rises higher than the second piece of tape, the object has greater volume than your fist. If the water level is lower, the object has less volume. Can you find a rock with the same volume as your fist? How about a potato? How many pennies does it take to reach the same volume as your fist?

Units of Measurement

Look at the shape to the right. It has four sides. And each side has a number that tells us its length. We can use these numbers to measure the **perimeter**—the distance around the outside of the shape. We can also use them to find the **area**—the space inside the shape. But what do these numbers mean?

Long ago, people didn't have rulers to help them measure things. So they used what they had—their arms, hands, and feet. But some people have longer arms, wider hands, or bigger feet than other people. So measurements using body parts didn't always match.

The Egyptian cubit was divided into measurements called digits and palms.

At some point, people decided to create standard measurements. That means measurements that are the same all the time.

Today, we can use several different standards of measurement. Many people in the United States use the inch-pound system. The inch-pound system includes inches, feet, yards, and miles for measuring length.

The metric system is used in most countries of the world. It includes millimeters, centimeters, meters, and kilometers for measuring length.

The units of measurement we use depend on the size of the object we're measuring. For example, you wouldn't use yards or meters to measure a paper clip! You'd need to use smaller units, such as centimeters or inches.

The Egyptian cubit was copied onto sticks so everyone could use it as a standard of measurement.

One millimeter: about the thickness of a paper match

One centimeter: about half the distance across a United States nickel

One meter: about the length of four pages of this book placed top-to-bottom

One kilometer: about the length of five city blocks

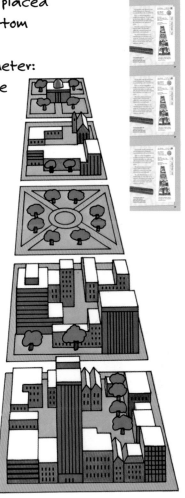

The metric system's values are based on 10's, using the decimal system.

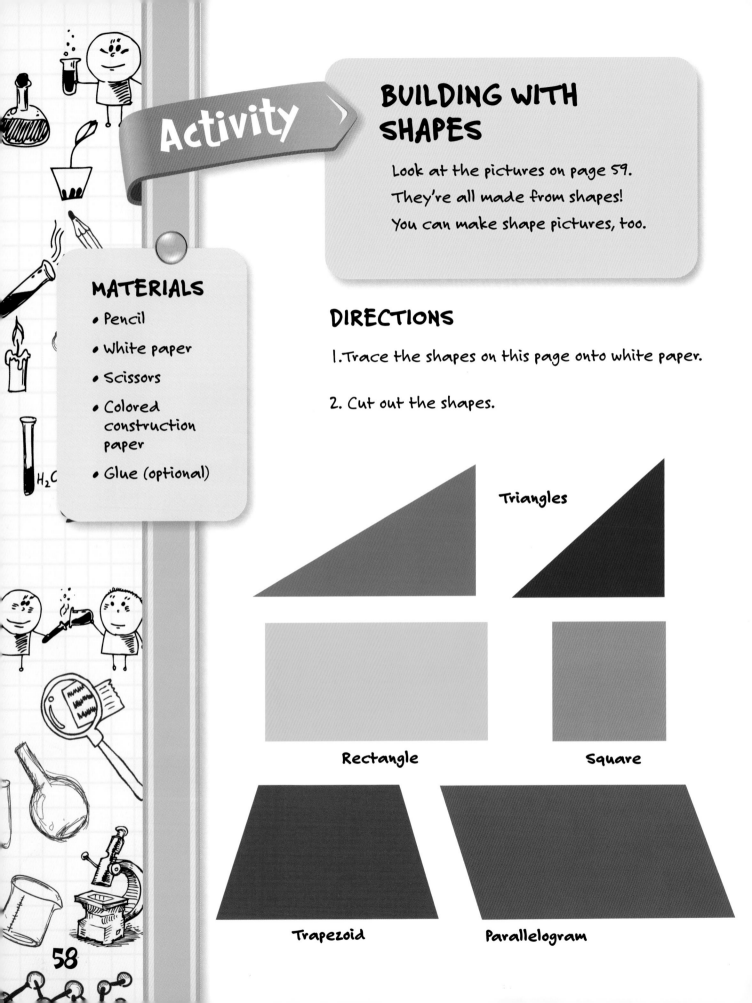

Activity

BUILDING WITH SHAPES

Look at the pictures on page 59. They're all made from shapes! You can make shape pictures, too.

MATERIALS

- Pencil
- White paper
- Scissors
- Colored construction paper
- Glue (optional)

DIRECTIONS

1. Trace the shapes on this page onto white paper.

2. Cut out the shapes.

Triangles

Rectangle

Square

Trapezoid

Parallelogram

H_2C

3. Lay the shapes on colored construction paper. Hold each shape down and carefully draw around it.

4. Cut out the colored shapes.

5. Repeat steps 3 and 4 to make lots of shapes in different colors.

6. Arrange some of your colored shapes on a piece of white paper. Follow the patterns shown on this page or design your own pictures.

7. If you want to keep a picture, glue the shapes onto the white paper.

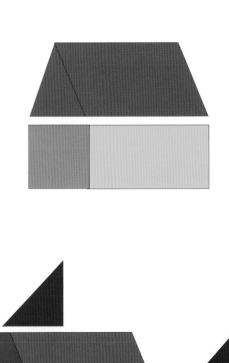

 **ANSWERS**

Pages 12-13—Edible Angles

1. 120 degrees is slice d,   90 degrees is slice a,   40 degrees is slice c,   20 degrees is slice b

2. 90 degrees

3. 120 degrees

Pages 16-17—Counting Triangles

They're all equilateral triangles.

Pages 20-21—Disappearing Squares

2. Here are four of the possible solutions. Take away the toothpicks shown in red.

3. Here are two possible solutions. Take away the toothpicks shown in red

5. Move the red toothpicks as shown.

a. 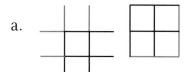   b. 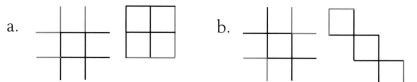   c.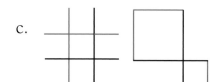

Pages 22-23—Polyominoes

Here is one way to make a 6 x 10 rectangle:

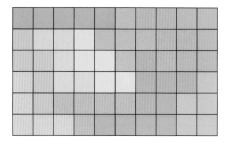

Here is one way to make a
5 x 12 rectangle:

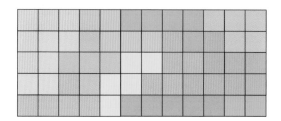

Pages 32-33—Lines of Symmetry

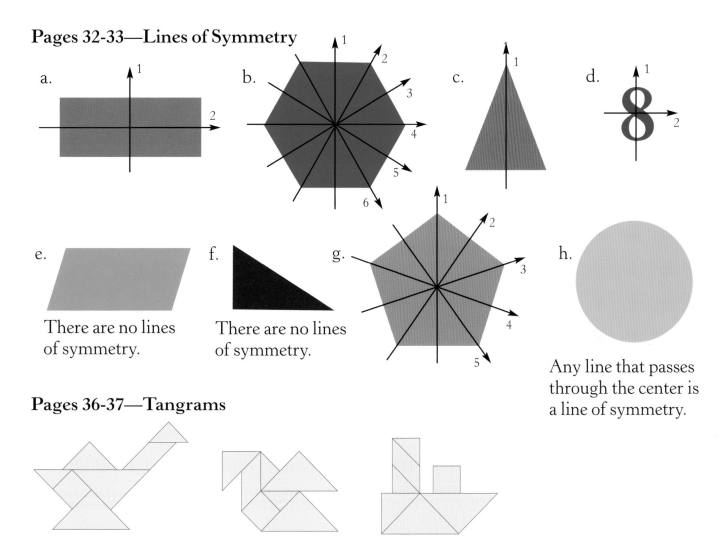

a.

b.

c.

d.

e. There are no lines of symmetry.

f. There are no lines of symmetry.

g.

h. Any line that passes through the center is a line of symmetry.

Pages 36-37—Tangrams

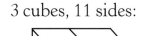

Pages 44-45—Congruent Shapes

1. a and e   2. There is one pair—b and e.   3. a and d are congruent shapes.

Pages 48-49—What Is the Area?

The area of the castle is 46 squares. The area of the skyscraper is 38 squares. The area of the castle is 8 squares larger.

Pages 50-51—What Is the Area?

1. 6 x 10 = 60   2. 5 x 5 = 25   3. 2 x 12 = 24   4. 3 x 6 = 18   5. 12 x 12 = 144

Pages 52—Solid Shapes

2 cubes, 8 sides: 3 cubes, 11 sides: 4 cubes, 12 sides:

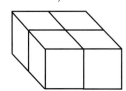

Glossary

acute angle an angle that has less than 90 degrees.

angle a figure formed by two lines that meet at a point.

area the space inside a flat shape.

circumference the distance around the boundary of a circle.

cylinder a solid shape. Its ends are two equal circles.

diameter a straight line passing from one side to the other through the center of a circle or sphere.

equilateral having all sides equal.

isosceles having two equal sides.

multiplication a fast way of adding numbers that are the same. A multiplication problem may look like this: $4 \times 2 = 8$.

obtuse angle an angle that has between 90 degrees and 180 degrees.

parallel being the same distance apart everywhere like the two rails of a straight railroad track.

parallelogram a flat, four-sided shape. Its opposite sides are the same length, and they are the same distance apart for all of their length.

perimeter the outer boundary of a shape.

polygon a flat shape with three or more straight sides.

protractor a device for measuring the size of angles or drawing angles.

quadrilateral a flat shape with four straight sides.

radius any line going straight from the center to the edge of a circle or sphere.

ray a line that goes on forever in one direction.

rhombus a parallelogram with equal sides, usually having two obtuse angles and two acute angles.

right angle an angle that has 90 degrees.

right triangle a triangle that has one 90-degree angle.

scalene a triangle that has three unequal sides.

sphere a perfectly round solid shape.

volume the amount of space inside a container or the amount a container will hold.

Find Out More

Books

Where We Play Sports: Measuring the Perimeters of Polygons by Greg Roza (PowerKids Press, 2004)

Measurement Mania: Games and Activities That Make Math Easy and Fun by Lynette Long (Wiley, 2001)

Volume by Chris Woodford (Blackbirch Press, 2005)

Circles and Spheres by Bonnie Coulter Leech (Rosen Publishing Group's PowerKids Press, 2007)

Triangles by Bonnie Coulter Leech (Rosen Publishing Group's PowerKids Press, 2007)

Polygons by Marina Cohen (Crabtree Publishing, 2011)

Websites

A+ Click
http://www.aplusclick.com/geometry.htm
Try to answer different questions about shapes, lines, and angles at this website.

AAA Math: Geometry
http://www.aaastudy.com/geo.htm
This site reviews the concepts of perimeter, area, circumference, and other ways of measuring and calculating shapes.

Math is Fun: Geometry
http://www.mathsisfun.com/geometry/index.html
This educational website will take you through the different types of geometry, as well as the basics of shapes and angles.

Cyberchase: Spaceship Builder
http://pbskids.org/cyberchase/games/perimeterarea/perimeterarea.html
In this online game, you will use lines and polygons to design spaceships for Dr. Marbles's new fleet.

The Math League: Geometry
http://www.themathleague.com/index.php?option=com_content&view=article&id=71&Itemid=67
Review angles, polygons, solids, and measurement at this educational website.

The National Library of Virtual Manipulatives: Geometry
http://nlvm.usu.edu/en/nav/topic_t_3.html
At this educational website, you can build congruent triangles, play around with trominoes and pentominoes, use geoboards to figure out area and perimeter, and have fun with fractals.

Tangrams
http://pbskids.org/sagwa/games/tangrams/index.html
Click and drag the seven tangram pieces to create pictures. Includes an easy level and a hard level.

Index

Activities